The Teacher Planner

By Ellen J. Rank

Calendars, Tools, and Templates for the Purposeful Jewish Educator

Name:

School/Education Program:

Year:

Behrman House
www.behrmanhouse.com

CONTENTS

מִתּוֹךְ שֶׁאַתָּה מְלַמֵּד, אַתָּה לָמֵד.

As you teach, you learn. — *Midrash T'hilim*

Book and cover design: Susan Neuhaus, Neustudio
Project Editor: Terry S. Kaye
Copyright © 2017 Behrman House, Inc.
Springfield, New Jersey
www.behrmanhouse.com

ISBN: 978-0-87441-997-9
Manufactured in the United States of America

IN ACTION

Preserving the Earth/*Bal Tashchit*   בַּל תַּשְׁחִית

Help students research how paper, plastic, cardboard, glass, cans, electronics, and food waste are recycled in their communities. Guide students as they plan and implement a recycling drive.

Doing Acts of Loving-kindness/*G'milut Chasadim*   גְּמִילוּת חֲסָדִים

Discuss opportunities for doing acts of loving-kindness, such as visiting the elderly or serving food at a soup kitchen. Accompany your students as they volunteer and engage in helping others.

Pursuing Peace/*R'difat Shalom*   רְדִיפַת שָׁלוֹם

Invite students to share times, such as making peace among friends, when they actively pursued peace. Encourage students to write out a personal commitment describing a way they can help bring more peace to the world.

Visiting the Sick/*Bikur Cholim*   בִּקּוּר חוֹלִים

Set up a *bikur cholim* rotation in your class. When a student is absent due to illness, the next student in the rotation will call or video chat to wish the classmate a quick recovery.

Loving Israel/*Ahavat Tziyon*   אַהֲבַת צִיּוֹן

Show a short video about one or more cities in Israel. In small groups, have students create a travel itinerary with descriptions of places they would like to visit in those cities.

Freeing Others/*Pidyon Sh'vuyim*   פִּדְיוֹן שְׁבוּיִים

Provide a letter template and encourage students to write to a politician in support of a particular person or group.

Studying Torah/*Talmud Torah*   תַּלְמוּד תּוֹרָה

Discuss how teaching is one of the best ways to learn. Invite students to describe ways that they can teach others. Arrange for your students to teach younger students. They might, for example, teach about a holiday or a new prayer.

Welcoming Guests/*Hachnasat Orchim*   הַכְנָסַת אוֹרְחִים

With your students, plan a Shabbat meal for their families. Have students write and send invitations, prepare the menu, cook and help serve the meal.

Peace in the Home/*Sh'lom Bayit*   שְׁלוֹם בַּיִת

Encourage students to make a personal commitment to do one new thing that can increase peace in their own homes. After a few weeks, discuss: Has it been hard or easy to do this? How does it make you feel? Has it made a difference?

Giving Justly/*Tzedakah*   צְדָקָה

Have the class research charitable organizations. In small groups, have students prepare posters reflecting the work of a charity of choice to encourage others to donate to this organization. Display the posters in the hallway.

Protecting Animals/*Tza'ar Ba'alei-Chayyim*   צַעַר בַּעֲלֵי-חַיִּים

Take your students on a visit to a local animal shelter. Bring items, such as blankets and towels, that can be used for animals in the shelter.

JEWISH AND SECULAR
CALENDAR
5778-85/2017-26

JEWISH YEAR	5778	5779	5780	5781	5782
SECULAR YEAR	2017	2018	2019	2020	2021
Labor Day	Sept 4	Sept 3	Sept 2	Sept 7	Sept 6
Rosh Hashanah	Sept 21, 22	Sept 10, 11	Sept 30, Oct 1	Sept 19, 20	Sept 7, 8
Yom Kippur	Sept 30	Sept 19	Oct 9	Sept 28	Sept 16
Sukkot	Oct 5, 6*	Sept 24, 25*	Oct 14, 15*	Oct 3, 4*	Sept 21, 22*
Shemini Atzeret	Oct 12	Oct 1	Oct 21	Oct 10	Sept 28
Simchat Torah	Oct 12**/13*	Oct 1**/2*	Oct 21**/22*	Oct 10**, 11*	Sept 28**, 29*
Thanksgiving	Nov 23	Nov 22	Nov 28	Nov 26	Nov 25
Hanukkah 1st candle (eve)	Dec 12	Dec 2	Dec 22	Dec 10	Nov 28
Christmas	Dec 25	Dec 25	Dec 25	Dec 25	Dec 25

	2018	2019	2020	2021	2022
New Year's Day	Jan 1	Jan 1	Jan 1	Jan 1	Jan 1
Martin Luther King Day	Jan 15	Jan 21	Jan 20	Jan 18	Jan 17
Tu BiShevat	Jan 31	Jan 21	Feb 10	Jan 28	Jan 17
Presidents' Day	Feb 19	Feb 18	Feb 17	Feb 15	Feb 21
Purim	March 1	March 21	March 10	Feb 26	March 17
Passover 1st seder (eve)	March 30	April 19	April 8	March 27	April 15
Passover, Days 1 and 2	March 31, April 1*	April 20, 21*	April 9, 10*	March 28, 29*	April 16, 17*
Passover, Days 7 and 8	April 6, 7*	April 26, 27*	April 15, 16*	April 3, 4*	April 22, 23*
Yom Hashoah	April 12	May 2	April 21	April 8	April 28
Yom Ha'atzma'ut	April 19	May 9	April 29	April 15	May 5
Lag Ba'omer	May 3	May 23	May 12	April 30	May 19
Shavuot	May 20, 21*	June 9, 10*	May 29, 30*	May 17, 18*	June 5, 6*
Memorial Day	May 28	May 27	May 25	May 31	May 30
Independence Day	July 4	July 4	July 4	July 4	July 4
Tisha B'Av	July 21	Aug 10	July 30	July 18	Aug 6

* Conservative   ** Reform

JEWISH YEAR	5783	5784	5785	5786
SECULAR YEAR	2022	2023	2024	2025
Labor Day	Sept 5	Sept 4	Sept 2	Sept 1
Rosh Hashanah	Sept 26, 27	Sept 16, 17	Oct 3, 4	Sept 23, 24
Yom Kippur	Oct 5	Sept 25	Oct 12	Oct 2
Sukkot	Oct 10, 11*	Sept 30, Oct 1*	Oct 17, 18*	Oct 7, 8*
Shemini Atzeret	Oct 17	Oct 7	Oct 24	Oct 14
Simchat Torah	Oct 17**, 18*	Oct 7**, 8*	Oct 24**, 25*	Oct 14**, 15*
Thanksgiving	Nov 24	Nov 23	Nov 28	Nov 27
Hanukkah 1st candle (eve)	Dec 18	Dec 7	Dec 25	Dec 14
Christmas	Dec 25	Dec 25	Dec 25	Dec 25
	2023	2024	2025	2026
New Year's Day	Jan 1	Jan 1	Jan 1	Jan 1
Martin Luther King Day	Jan 16	Jan 15	Jan 20	Jan 19
Tu BiShevat	Feb 6	Jan 25	Feb 13	Feb 2
Presidents' Day	Feb 20	Feb 19	Feb 17	Feb 16
Purim	March 7	March 24	March 14	March 3
Passover 1st seder (eve)	April 5	April 22	April 12	April 1
Passover, Days 1 and 2	April 6, 7*	April 23, 24*	April 13, 14*	April 2, 3*
Passover, Days 7 and 8	April 12, 13*	April 29, 30*	April 19, 20*	April 8, 9*
Yom Hashoah	April 18	May 6	April 24	April 14
Yom Ha'atzma'ut	April 26	May 14	May 1	April 22
Lag Ba'omer	May 9	May 26	May 16	May 5
Shavuot	May 26, 27*	June 12, 13*	June 2, 3*	May 22, 23*
Memorial Day	May 29	May 27	May 26	May 25
Independence Day	July 4	July 4	July 4	July 4
Tisha B'Av	July 27	Aug 13	Aug 3	July 23

* Conservative   ** Reform

What happened this week that you are most proud of?

YEARLY
CALENDAR

Attach this year's school calendar to these pages. Use the chart to note important dates and reminders.

August

September

October

November

December

January

February

March

April

May

June

STUDENT  AND PARENT/GUARDIAN CONTACT

Attach your student rosters with contact information to these pages. Use the chart to keep a record of your communications with parents or guardians.

	STUDENT'S NAME	DATE	PARENT/ GUARDIAN CONTACTED	REASON FOR CONTACT	NEXT STEPS OR REFLECTIONS
1					
2					
3					
4					
5					
6					
7					
8					
9					
10					
11					
12					

אִם אֵין אֲנִי לִי, מִי לִי? וּכְשֶׁאֲנִי לְעַצְמִי, מָה אֲנִי?

If I am not for myself, who will be? And if I am only for myself, what am I? — *Avot 1:14*

	STUDENT'S NAME	DATE	PARENT/ GUARDIAN CONTACTED	REASON FOR CONTACT	NEXT STEPS OR REFLECTIONS
13					
14					
15					
16					
17					
18					
19					
20					
21					
22					
23					
24					

Add each child's birthday to your roster. Give them a special wish that day.

ATTENDANCE

Class/Group_____

P = Present   A = Absent   L = Late arrival   E = Early leaving

	STUDENT'S NAME	1	2	3	4	5	6	7	8	9	10	11	12	13	14	15	16	17	18	19	20	21	22	23	24	25
1																										
2																										
3																										
4																										
5																										
6																										
7																										
8																										
9																										
10																										
11																										
12																										
13																										
14																										
15																										
16																										
17																										
18																										
19																										
20																										
21																										
22																										
23																										
24																										
25																										

הֱוֵי מַקְדִּים בְּשָׁלוֹם כָּל אָדָם.

Be the first to greet every person. — *Avot 4:20*

26	27	28	29	30	31	32	33	34	35	36	37	38	39	40	41	42	43	44	45	46	47	48	49	50	NOTES	
																										1
																										2
																										3
																										4
																										5
																										6
																										7
																										8
																										9
																										10
																										11
																										12
																										13
																										14
																										15
																										16
																										17
																										18
																										19
																										20
																										21
																										22
																										23
																										24
																										25

ATTENDANCE

Class/Group_____

P = Present   A = Absent   L = Late arrival   E = Early leaving

	STUDENT'S NAME	1	2	3	4	5	6	7	8	9	10	11	12	13	14	15	16	17	18	19	20	21	22	23	24	25
1																										
2																										
3																										
4																										
5																										
6																										
7																										
8																										
9																										
10																										
11																										
12																										
13																										
14																										
15																										
16																										
17																										
18																										
19																										
20																										
21																										
22																										
23																										
24																										
25																										

וֶהֱוֵי מְקַבֵּל אֶת כָּל הָאָדָם בְּשִׂמְחָה.

Greet every person with joy. — *Avot 3:16*

26	27	28	29	30	31	32	33	34	35	36	37	38	39	40	41	42	43	44	45	46	47	48	49	50	Notes	
																										1
																										2
																										3
																										4
																										5
																										6
																										7
																										8
																										9
																										10
																										11
																										12
																										13
																										14
																										15
																										16
																										17
																										18
																										19
																										20
																										21
																										22
																										23
																										24
																										25

Center yourself by taking a slow, deep breath.

ASSESSMENT

Class/Group _____

Use these pages to record student progress. In the top row, briefly describe the activity you are assessing.

ACTIVITY / STUDENT'S NAME								
1								
2								
3								
4								
5								
6								
7								
8								
9								
10								
11								
12								
13								
14								
15								
16								
17								
18								
19								
20								

בִּשְׁבִיל הַחֶסֶד הָעוֹלָם מִתְקַיֵּם.

The world exists for the sake of kindness. — *Rashi on Avot 1:2*

NOTES

1
2
3
4
5
6
7
8
9
10
11
12
13
14
15
16
17
18
19
20

Class/Group_____

Use these pages to record student progress. In the top row, briefly describe the activity you are assessing.

ACTIVITY STUDENT'S NAME								
1								
2								
3								
4								
5								
6								
7								
8								
9								
10								
11								
12								
13								
14								
15								
16								
17								
18								
19								
20								

In Judaism, to be without questions is not
a sign of faith, but of lack of depth.
— *Rabbi Lord Jonathan Sacks*

NOTES

1

2

3

4

5

6

7

8

9

10

11

12

13

14

15

16

17

18

19

20

What happened in a lesson today that surprised you?

GOALS

GOAL 1 A personal or professional goal
I have for this year is:

This goal is important to me because:

Some people who can help me reach the goal are:

I can measure my progress by:

3 steps I will take to reach this goal are:

1.
2.
3.

When I reach this goal I:

GOAL 2 A personal or professional goal
I have for this year is:

This goal is important to me because:

Some people who can help me reach the goal are:

I can measure my progress by:

3 steps I will take to reach this goal are:

1.
2.
3.

When I reach this goal I:

GOAL 3 A personal or professional goal
I have for this year is:

This goal is important to me because:

Some people who can help me reach the goal are:

I can measure my progress by:

3 steps I will take to reach this goal are:

1.
2.
3.

When I reach this goal I:

How Am I Doing?

1

	Mid-Year Check In	End-of-Year Check In
To reach this goal I have:		
People and experiences that helped me:		
Now I would like to:		
How I feel about my progress (circle one):		

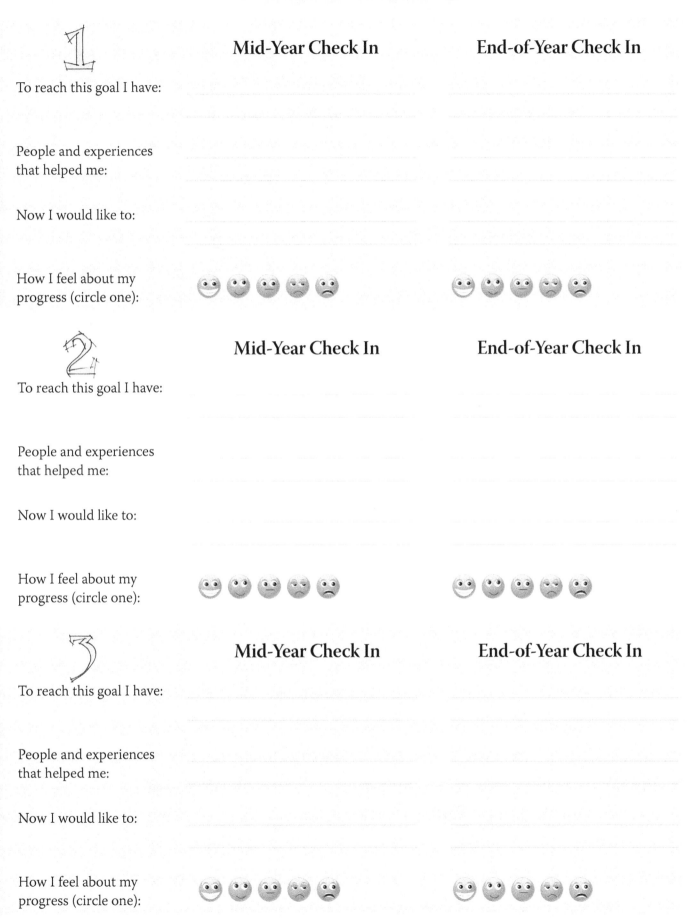

2

	Mid-Year Check In	End-of-Year Check In
To reach this goal I have:		
People and experiences that helped me:		
Now I would like to:		
How I feel about my progress (circle one):		

3

	Mid-Year Check In	End-of-Year Check In
To reach this goal I have:		
People and experiences that helped me:		
Now I would like to:		
How I feel about my progress (circle one):		

LESSON 1

Class/Group:

Learner Goals:

Lesson Structure, Activities, Time:

Materials:

Reflections:

Reminders
(special needs, homework, events)

LESSON 2

Class/Group:

Learner Goals:

Lesson Structure, Activities, Time:

Materials:

Reflections:

Reminders
(special needs, homework, events)

LESSON 3

Class/Group:

Learner Goals:

Lesson Structure, Activities, Time:

Materials:

Reflections:

Reminders
(special needs, homework, events)

LESSON 1

Class/Group:

Learner Goals:

Lesson Structure, Activities, Time:

Materials:

Reflections:

Reminders
(special needs, homework, events)

LESSON 2

Class/Group:

Learner Goals:

Lesson Structure, Activities, Time:

Materials:

Reflections:

Reminders
(special needs, homework, events)

LESSON 3

Class/Group:

Learner Goals:

Lesson Structure, Activities, Time:

Materials:

Reflections:

Reminders
(special needs, homework, events)

PLAN for week of

Class/Group:

Learner Goals:

Lesson Structure, Activities, Time:

Materials:

Reflections:

Reminders
(special needs, homework, events)

Class/Group:

Learner Goals:

Lesson Structure, Activities, Time:

Materials:

Reflections:

Reminders
(special needs, homework, events)

Class/Group:

Learner Goals:

Lesson Structure, Activities, Time:

Materials:

Reflections:

Reminders
(special needs, homework, events)

PLAN for week of

LESSON 1

Class/Group:

Learner Goals:

Lesson Structure, Activities, Time:

Materials:

Reflections:

Reminders
(special needs, homework, events)

LESSON 2

Class/Group:

Learner Goals:

Lesson Structure, Activities, Time:

Materials:

Reflections:

Reminders
(special needs, homework, events)

LESSON 3

Class/Group:

Learner Goals:

Lesson Structure, Activities, Time:

Materials:

Reflections:

Reminders
(special needs, homework, events)

PLAN for week of

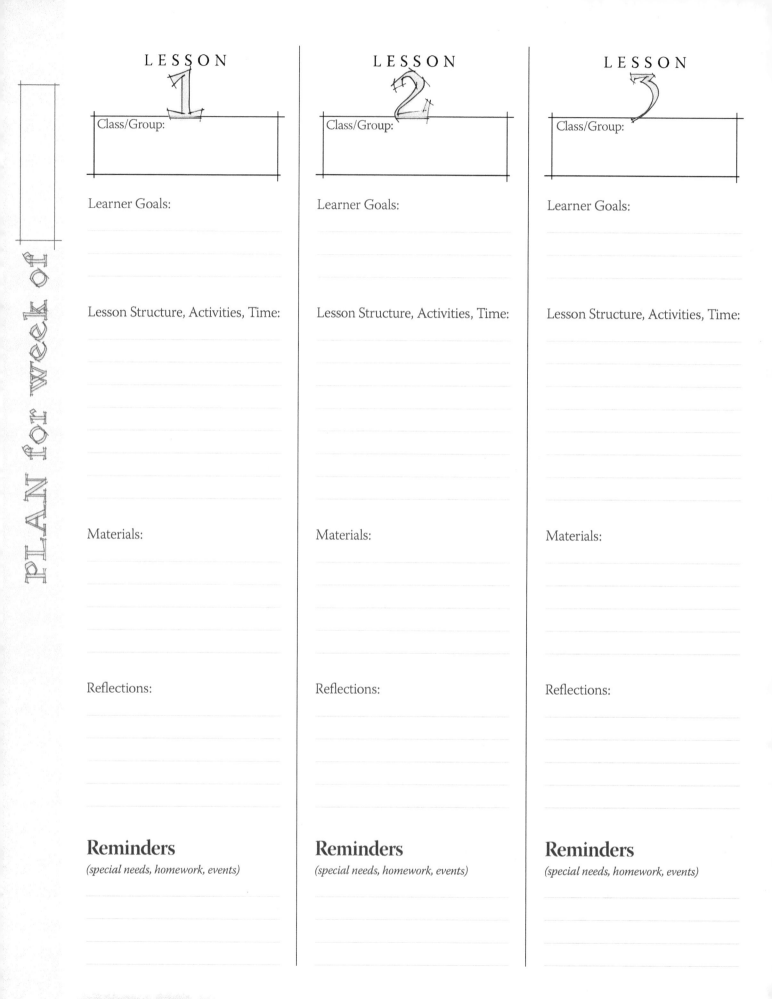

PLAN for week of

LESSON 1

Class/Group:

Learner Goals:

Lesson Structure, Activities, Time:

Materials:

Reflections:

Reminders
(special needs, homework, events)

LESSON 2

Class/Group:

Learner Goals:

Lesson Structure, Activities, Time:

Materials:

Reflections:

Reminders
(special needs, homework, events)

LESSON 3

Class/Group:

Learner Goals:

Lesson Structure, Activities, Time:

Materials:

Reflections:

Reminders
(special needs, homework, events)

LESSON 1

Class/Group:

Learner Goals:

Lesson Structure, Activities, Time:

Materials:

Reflections:

Reminders
(special needs, homework, events)

LESSON 2

Class/Group:

Learner Goals:

Lesson Structure, Activities, Time:

Materials:

Reflections:

Reminders
(special needs, homework, events)

LESSON 3

Class/Group:

Learner Goals:

Lesson Structure, Activities, Time:

Materials:

Reflections:

Reminders
(special needs, homework, events)

PLAN for week of

LESSON 1

Class/Group:

Learner Goals:

Lesson Structure, Activities, Time:

Materials:

Reflections:

Reminders
(special needs, homework, events)

LESSON 2

Class/Group:

Learner Goals:

Lesson Structure, Activities, Time:

Materials:

Reflections:

Reminders
(special needs, homework, events)

LESSON 3

Class/Group:

Learner Goals:

Lesson Structure, Activities, Time:

Materials:

Reflections:

Reminders
(special needs, homework, events)

L E S S O N 1

Class/Group:

Learner Goals:

Lesson Structure, Activities, Time:

Materials:

Reflections:

Reminders

(special needs, homework, events)

L E S S O N 2

Class/Group:

Learner Goals:

Lesson Structure, Activities, Time:

Materials:

Reflections:

Reminders

(special needs, homework, events)

L E S S O N 3

Class/Group:

Learner Goals:

Lesson Structure, Activities, Time:

Materials:

Reflections:

Reminders

(special needs, homework, events)

PLAN for week of

LESSON 1

Class/Group:

Learner Goals:

Lesson Structure, Activities, Time:

Materials:

Reflections:

Reminders
(special needs, homework, events)

LESSON 2

Class/Group:

Learner Goals:

Lesson Structure, Activities, Time:

Materials:

Reflections:

Reminders
(special needs, homework, events)

LESSON 3

Class/Group:

Learner Goals:

Lesson Structure, Activities, Time:

Materials:

Reflections:

Reminders
(special needs, homework, events)

LESSON 1

Class/Group:

Learner Goals:

Lesson Structure, Activities, Time:

Materials:

Reflections:

Reminders
(special needs, homework, events)

LESSON 2

Class/Group:

Learner Goals:

Lesson Structure, Activities, Time:

Materials:

Reflections:

Reminders
(special needs, homework, events)

LESSON 3

Class/Group:

Learner Goals:

Lesson Structure, Activities, Time:

Materials:

Reflections:

Reminders
(special needs, homework, events)

PLAN for week of

LESSON 1

Class/Group:

Learner Goals:

Lesson Structure, Activities, Time:

Materials:

Reflections:

Reminders
(special needs, homework, events)

LESSON 2

Class/Group:

Learner Goals:

Lesson Structure, Activities, Time:

Materials:

Reflections:

Reminders
(special needs, homework, events)

LESSON 3

Class/Group:

Learner Goals:

Lesson Structure, Activities, Time:

Materials:

Reflections:

Reminders
(special needs, homework, events)

LESSON 1

Class/Group:

Learner Goals:

Lesson Structure, Activities, Time:

Materials:

Reflections:

Reminders
(special needs, homework, events)

LESSON 2

Class/Group:

Learner Goals:

Lesson Structure, Activities, Time:

Materials:

Reflections:

Reminders
(special needs, homework, events)

LESSON 3

Class/Group:

Learner Goals:

Lesson Structure, Activities, Time:

Materials:

Reflections:

Reminders
(special needs, homework, events)

PLAN for week of

PLAN for week of

LESSON 1

Class/Group:

Learner Goals:

Lesson Structure, Activities, Time:

Materials:

Reflections:

Reminders
(special needs, homework, events)

LESSON 2

Class/Group:

Learner Goals:

Lesson Structure, Activities, Time:

Materials:

Reflections:

Reminders
(special needs, homework, events)

LESSON 3

Class/Group:

Learner Goals:

Lesson Structure, Activities, Time:

Materials:

Reflections:

Reminders
(special needs, homework, events)

LESSON 1

Class/Group:

Learner Goals:

Lesson Structure, Activities, Time:

Materials:

Reflections:

Reminders
(special needs, homework, events)

LESSON 2

Class/Group:

Learner Goals:

Lesson Structure, Activities, Time:

Materials:

Reflections:

Reminders
(special needs, homework, events)

LESSON 3

Class/Group:

Learner Goals:

Lesson Structure, Activities, Time:

Materials:

Reflections:

Reminders
(special needs, homework, events)

PLAN for week of

LESSON 1

Class/Group:

Learner Goals:

Lesson Structure, Activities, Time:

Materials:

Reflections:

Reminders
(special needs, homework, events)

LESSON 2

Class/Group:

Learner Goals:

Lesson Structure, Activities, Time:

Materials:

Reflections:

Reminders
(special needs, homework, events)

LESSON 3

Class/Group:

Learner Goals:

Lesson Structure, Activities, Time:

Materials:

Reflections:

Reminders
(special needs, homework, events)

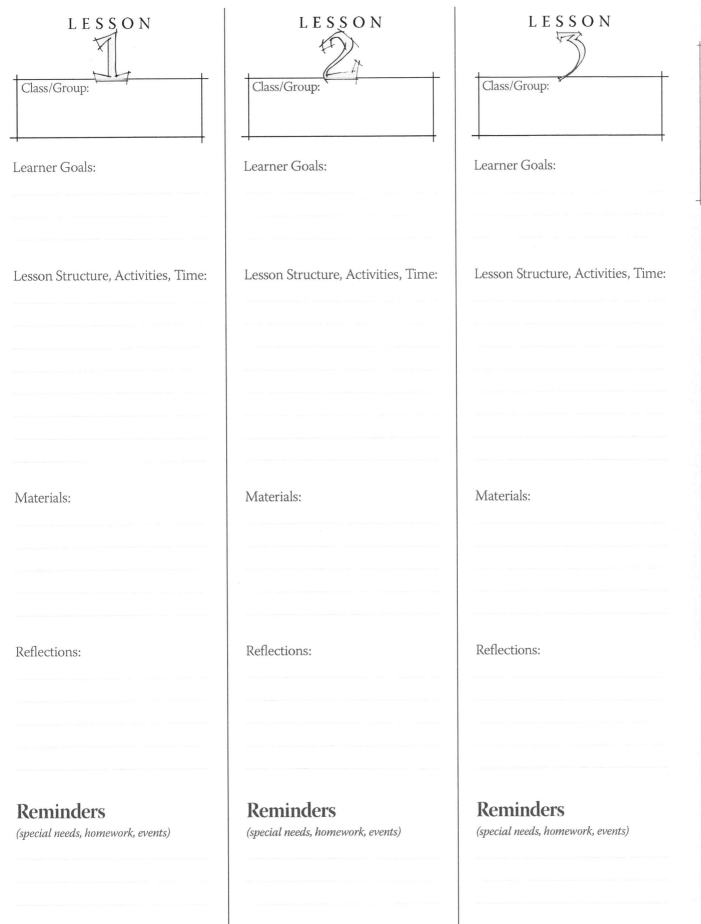

L E S S O N 1

Class/Group:

Learner Goals:

Lesson Structure, Activities, Time:

Materials:

Reflections:

Reminders
(special needs, homework, events)

L E S S O N 2

Class/Group:

Learner Goals:

Lesson Structure, Activities, Time:

Materials:

Reflections:

Reminders
(special needs, homework, events)

L E S S O N 3

Class/Group:

Learner Goals:

Lesson Structure, Activities, Time:

Materials:

Reflections:

Reminders
(special needs, homework, events)

PLAN for week of

PLAN for week of

LESSON 1

Class/Group:

Learner Goals:

Lesson Structure, Activities, Time:

Materials:

Reflections:

Reminders
(special needs, homework, events)

LESSON 2

Class/Group:

Learner Goals:

Lesson Structure, Activities, Time:

Materials:

Reflections:

Reminders
(special needs, homework, events)

LESSON 3

Class/Group:

Learner Goals:

Lesson Structure, Activities, Time:

Materials:

Reflections:

Reminders
(special needs, homework, events)

LESSON 1

Class/Group:

Learner Goals:

Lesson Structure, Activities, Time:

Materials:

Reflections:

Reminders
(special needs, homework, events)

LESSON 2

Class/Group:

Learner Goals:

Lesson Structure, Activities, Time:

Materials:

Reflections:

Reminders
(special needs, homework, events)

LESSON 3

Class/Group:

Learner Goals:

Lesson Structure, Activities, Time:

Materials:

Reflections:

Reminders
(special needs, homework, events)

Take a break: Doodle mindlessly in the margins.

PLAN for week of

Class/Group:

Learner Goals:

Lesson Structure, Activities, Time:

Materials:

Reflections:

Reminders
(special needs, homework, events)

Class/Group:

Learner Goals:

Lesson Structure, Activities, Time:

Materials:

Reflections:

Reminders
(special needs, homework, events)

Class/Group:

Learner Goals:

Lesson Structure, Activities, Time:

Materials:

Reflections:

Reminders
(special needs, homework, events)

PLAN for week of

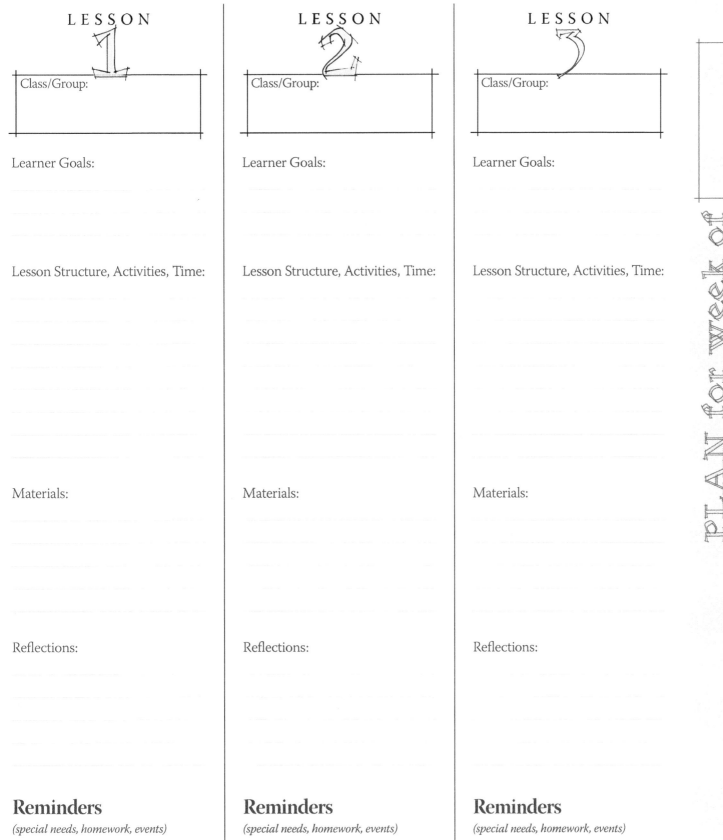

LESSON 1

Class/Group:

Learner Goals:

Lesson Structure, Activities, Time:

Materials:

Reflections:

Reminders
(special needs, homework, events)

LESSON 2

Class/Group:

Learner Goals:

Lesson Structure, Activities, Time:

Materials:

Reflections:

Reminders
(special needs, homework, events)

LESSON 3

Class/Group:

Learner Goals:

Lesson Structure, Activities, Time:

Materials:

Reflections:

Reminders
(special needs, homework, events)

PLAN for week of

PLAN for week of

LESSON 1

Class/Group:

Learner Goals:

Lesson Structure, Activities, Time:

Materials:

Reflections:

Reminders
(special needs, homework, events)

LESSON 2

Class/Group:

Learner Goals:

Lesson Structure, Activities, Time:

Materials:

Reflections:

Reminders
(special needs, homework, events)

LESSON 3

Class/Group:

Learner Goals:

Lesson Structure, Activities, Time:

Materials:

Reflections:

Reminders
(special needs, homework, events)

LESSON 1

Class/Group:

Learner Goals:

Lesson Structure, Activities, Time:

Materials:

Reflections:

Reminders
(special needs, homework, events)

LESSON 2

Class/Group:

Learner Goals:

Lesson Structure, Activities, Time:

Materials:

Reflections:

Reminders
(special needs, homework, events)

LESSON 3

Class/Group:

Learner Goals:

Lesson Structure, Activities, Time:

Materials:

Reflections:

Reminders
(special needs, homework, events)

PLAN for week of

LESSON 1

Class/Group:

Learner Goals:

Lesson Structure, Activities, Time:

Materials:

Reflections:

Reminders
(special needs, homework, events)

LESSON 2

Class/Group:

Learner Goals:

Lesson Structure, Activities, Time:

Materials:

Reflections:

Reminders
(special needs, homework, events)

LESSON 3

Class/Group:

Learner Goals:

Lesson Structure, Activities, Time:

Materials:

Reflections:

Reminders
(special needs, homework, events)

LESSON 1

Class/Group:

Learner Goals:

Lesson Structure, Activities, Time:

Materials:

Reflections:

Reminders
(special needs, homework, events)

LESSON 2

Class/Group:

Learner Goals:

Lesson Structure, Activities, Time:

Materials:

Reflections:

Reminders
(special needs, homework, events)

LESSON 3

Class/Group:

Learner Goals:

Lesson Structure, Activities, Time:

Materials:

Reflections:

Reminders
(special needs, homework, events)

PLAN for week of

MINDFULNESS
FOR THE JEWISH EDUCATOR

Adapted from "Jewish Mindfulness in Prayer" by Rabbi Jill Berkson Zimmerman,
Hebrew in Harmony Curriculum Core, Behrman House

Mindfulness is the ability to pay attention to the present moment. We can be mindful about both mundane and sacred activities: washing the dishes, praying, brushing our teeth, or studying holy texts. For example, instead of brushing your teeth quickly while focusing on a to-do list, you can set an intention to brush your teeth, noticing the taste of the toothpaste, the feel of the bristles on your gums, and the sound of the motions. In every activity we do, we can choose to be in either a mindful state or a distracted one.

Sitting quietly (meditation), yoga, prayer, and intention-setting are all examples of practices that can help us cultivate mindfulness. Learning how to be still, cultivating compassion for ourselves and others, heightening gratitude and awe, and bringing calm into our lives are other ways we can become more mindful. Mindfulness is a way of being in the world that both adults and children can learn.

SIMPLE TECHNIQUES FOR PRACTICING MINDFULNESS

Breathing

Sit in a chair in a quiet place. Close your eyes and sit up straight, while still feeling relaxed. Feel your body sitting on the chair. Notice your breath, without forcing it in any way. For the next fifteen seconds, just pay attention to your breath as it moves in and out of your body. You may notice that your mind starts thinking about other things. That's okay. Gently come back to paying attention to your breath. Let your thoughts come and go without judging them or yourself.

You may find it helpful to use a timer. As you repeat the practice, increase the time from fifteen seconds to thirty or sixty or more. Ask yourself: "How was that experience? Where did I most notice the inhale and exhale? Did I notice my mind wandering? Was I able to remind myself to come back gently to my breath? How?" Wherever you are, you can bring this idea to anything you set as an intention.

Noticing Physical Sensations

When you get very still, you will be able to notice sensations in your body: tightness in your shoulders, a tingling of your nose, your feet firmly planted on the floor. Consciously relax by focusing on the tense parts of your body while you take a few deep breaths.

Listening

Try a listening activity. What sounds do you hear around you? Keep listening. When your mind wanders, bring yourself gently back to listening. When a new sound arises, pay attention to that sound. See if you can become especially attuned to listening.

What did you notice about the sounds? Did you hear sounds that you had never noticed before, such as the radiator, an airplane overhead, or traffic outside? Did you hear the sound of your own breath? What was easy or difficult about just listening?

Do this for around sixty seconds or more if you are able. This is an especially wonderful activity to do when it's raining or windy or where there are birds singing.

Consider the kind of attention it requires to listen only to sounds and what is required for really listening to our friends or family. How can you remind yourself to be a better listener?

Practicing Compassion

Try to focus on positive thoughts and emotions—for yourself and others. Smile. Privately, wish yourself to be safe and happy; wish the same for others. Think, "I wish that ___ [name] will be safe and happy." Imagine yourself doing generous acts for others and how this makes them feel. Such positive feelings can help you relate to others and yourself with kindness and acceptance.

Praying with Kavanah

Kavanah is about intentionality, directing our hearts and minds to a particular focus, whether on our breath, the sounds around us, or the words of prayer. Having *kavanah* or setting a *kavanah* is the opposite of "going on automatic." When we memorize our prayers, we may slip into reciting them by rote, forgetting the meaning of the words. Before the start of a prayer experience, sit quietly and set a *kavanah* for it; for example, "In today's service, I will pay attention to my own experience of the prayers we are saying," or, "Today I intend to say the Sh'ma slowly and pay close attention to each word."

Being mindful in your personal and professional life can help you identify your emotions, give you more choice about how you will react, and ultimately lead you toward a greater sense of well-being.

HEBREW AT A GLANCE

NUMBERS

4	3	2	1	0
אַרְבַּע	שָׁלֹשׁ	שְׁתַּיִם	אַחַת	אֶפֶס
arba	*shalosh*	*sh'tayim*	*achat*	*efes*
9	8	7	6	5
תֵּשַׁע	שְׁמוֹנֶה	שֶׁבַע	שֵׁשׁ	חָמֵשׁ
teisha	*sh'moneh*	*sheva*	*sheish*	*chameish*
100	20	12	11	10
מֵאָה	עֶשְׂרִים	שְׁתֵּים עֶשְׂרֵה	אַחַת עֶשְׂרֵה	עֶשֶׂר
mei'ah	*esrim*	*sh'teim esreih*	*achat esreih*	*eser*

DAYS OF THE WEEK

Sunday	*yom rishon*	יוֹם רִאשׁוֹן
Monday	*yom sheini*	יוֹם שֵׁנִי
Tuesday	*yom sh'lishi*	יוֹם שְׁלִישִׁי
Wednesday	*yom r'vi'i*	יוֹם רְבִיעִי
Thursday	*yom chamishi*	יוֹם חֲמִישִׁי
Friday	*yom shishi*	יוֹם שִׁשִׁי
Shabbat	*Shabbat*	יוֹם שַׁבָּת

COLORS

red	*adom*	אָדֹם
orange	*katom*	כָּתֹם
yellow	*tzahov*	צָהֹב
green	*yarok*	יָרֹק
blue	*kachol*	כָּחֹל
purple	*sagol*	סָגֹל
black	*shachor*	שָׁחֹר
white	*lavan*	לָבָן

HELPFUL HEBREW WORDS AND PHRASES

yes	ken	כֵּן
no	lo	לֹא
please, you're welcome	b'vakashah	בְּבַקָשָׁה
thank you	todah	תּוֹדָה
How are you?	mah sh'lom'cha? (m, sing.)	מַה שְׁלוֹמְךָ?
	mah sh'lomeich? (f, sing.)	מַה שְׁלוֹמֵךְ?
okay, fine	b'seder	בְּסֵדֶר
very good	tov m'od	טוֹב מְאֹד
so-so	kachah kachah	כָּכָה כָּכָה
not well (good)	lo tov	לֹא טוֹב
What is your name?	mah shimcha? (m, sing.)	מַה שְׁמְךָ?
	mah shmeich? (f, sing.)	מַה שְׁמֵךְ?
my name (is)	sh'mi	שְׁמִי
pleased to meet you	na'im m'od	נָעִים מְאֹד
see you soon	l'hit'ra'ot	לְהִתְרָאוֹת
who	mi	מִי
what	mah	מַה
where	eifoh	אֵיפֹה
in, in the	b', ba	בְּ-, בַּ-
to, to the	l', la	לְ-, לַ-
the	ha	הַ-
to sit	lashevet	לָשֶׁבֶת
to stand up	lakum	לָקוּם

IN THE CLASSROOM

teacher	moreh (m)	מוֹרֶה
	morah (f)	מוֹרָה
student	talmid (m)	תַּלְמִיד
	talmidah (f)	תַּלְמִידָה
	talmidim (m, pl.)	תַּלְמִידִים
friend	chaveir (m)	חָבֵר
	chaveirah (f)	חֲבֵרָה
	chaveirim (m, pl.)	חֲבֵרִים
class, classroom	kitah	כִּתָּה
door	delet	דֶּלֶת
window	chalon	חַלּוֹן
wall	kir	קִיר
chair	kisei	כִּסֵּא
table, desk	shulchan	שֻׁלְחָן
board, calendar	lu'ach	לוּחַ
notebook	machberet	מַחְבֶּרֶת
book	sefer	סֵפֶר
pencil	iparon	עִפָּרוֹן
pen	et	עֵט
chalk	gir	גִּיר
marker	toosh	טוּשׁ
eraser	machak	מַחַק
computer	machsheiv	מַחְשֵׁב
cellphone	pelefon, nayad, s'martfon	פֶּלָאפוֹן, נַיָּד, סְמַרְטְפוֹן
backpack	tik	תִּיק
water	mayim	מַיִם

ALEF-BET CHART

LETTERS

ה	ד	ג	ב	בּ	א
Hay	Dalet	Gimmel	Vet	Bet	Alef
כּ	י	ט	ח	ז	ו
Kaf	Yud	Tet	Chet	Zayin	Vav
נ	ם	מ	ל	ך	כ
Nun	Final Mem	Mem	Lamed	Final Chaf	Chaf
ף	פ	פּ	ע	ס	ן
Final Fay	Fay	Pay	Ayin	Samech	Final Nun
שׂ	שׁ	ר	ק	ץ	צ
Sin	Shin	Resh	Kuf	Final Tzadi	Tzadi
				תּ	ת
				Tav	Tav

VOWELS

chirik "ee" ·	chataf-patach ־ֲ "ah"	sh'va "uh" or no sound ְ	patach "ah" ־	kamatz "ah" ָ
chataf-segol "eh" ֱ	segol "eh" ֶ	chataf-kamatz ֳ "oh"	cholam-chaseir "oh" ·	cholam "oh" וֹ
	kubutz "oo" ֻ		shuruk "oo" וּ	tzeirei "ei" ֵ

Printed in the USA
CPSIA information can be obtained
at www.ICGtesting.com
JSHW060049150824
68134JS00031B/2687